is t   urne on c

STYLE BLITZ

STYLE BLITZ

Grooming and Good Looks for Boys

HELEN THORNE

Illustrated by Rachel Busch

Piccadilly Press • London

To Nicky

Acknowledgements:
The author would like to thank the boys of Bow
School who answered detailed questionnaires to
help with the research of this book.

Text copyright © Helen Thorne, 1994
Illustration copyright © Rachel Busch, 1994

The right of Helen Thorne to be identified as Author of this work
and Rachel Busch to be identified as Illustrator of this work has
been asserted by them in accordance with the Copyright, Designs
and Patents Act 1988.

Phototypeset from author's disk by Ruth Williams
Printed and bound by Biddles Ltd., Guildford
for the publishers Piccadilly Press Ltd.,
5 Castle Road, London NW1 8PR

A catalogue record for this book is available
from the British Library

ISBN: 1 85340 178 1 (hardback)
1 85340 183 8 (trade paperback)

Helen Thorne lives in East London. After graduating from the
London College of Fashion she worked as fashion reporter and
stylist on a number of newspapers and magazines including the
Daily Mirror, Just Seventeen and the *Independent.* She has
worked as a costume designer on several television shows and
feature films, and as a fashion presenter on programmes which
include *This Morning* and *Good Morning With Anne and Nick.*
She is currently presenting her fourth series for Yorkshire TV's
award-winning fashion programme, *The Calender Fashion Show.*

CONTENTS

WHAT IS 'GOOD LOOKING' ANYWAY?

A lot of boys are quite happy to give the impression that personal appearance is something of a taboo subject. Having a healthy interest in how you look is a definite no-no. And when it comes to actually using stuff like conditioners, cleansers and concealers, well sorry, it's a no-can-do situation.

But in reality, given half the chance, these very same lads are desperate to know how to look good and take pride in their appearance. It's only pressure from others that makes them utter such fibs as 'I can't remember the last time I looked in the mirror.' Whether we realise it or not, we are all concerned with physical perfection and image.

If the truth be known, when it comes to vanity boys and girls are equal. After all, why should wanting to look and feel as good as possible be a woman's prerogative?

Every boy wants to believe that he is going to

emerge from being a geeky, uncomfortable adolescent into God's gift to girls without any effort or assistance.

When you're young your parents teach and remind you to do things like brushing your teeth, scrubbing the back of your neck and cleaning the crop of potatoes that is growing between your toes. But just when you've got the hang of all that stuff, your body really begins to change.

It's a cruel twist of fate that, at the exact same time you start to care and are most conscious of the way you look, you are also most likely to have problems. The experience of a bad complexion, armpit odour and hair hassle all on the same

Monday morning makes you want to dive for cover under the nearest duvet.

It's seriously scary but at least that goes for everybody. However, this book is here to help. It's here to take you on a journey through your bathroom cabinet, guide you at the hairdresser and rifle through your sock drawer. It's a fool-proof manual for when you go travelling up and down the aisle of the local chemists.

There are loads of brilliant image-changing tips and tricks to try – and experimenting is the only way to discover what's going to work for you. So if you're ready to tackle that alluring array of sprays, soothers, scrubs and soaps, read on ...

Chapter One

GETTING TO GRIPS WITH WHAT YOU'VE GOT

We all have the potential to be pretty amazing looking. You can be as fit, as vital and as aware as you want to be. But if you spend your life comparing your looks to other people's, it's not surprising that you are left feeling miserable and with a pretty dim view of your own appearance. Even the rich and famous, the handsome and successful have self-doubts and insecurities ...

"I've always thought of myself as small. Geeky. Ferret-like."
Michael J Fox

"I don't even like wearing swimming trunks. Whenever my legs are on camera I try and make sure they're filmed from the best possible angle."
Baywatch star, David Hasselhoff

"On a scale of one to ten for my looks, I'd say I was

a one."
Gary Stretch

So it seems having a dollar-fat Hollywood contract, tens of thousands of adoring fans, and models for girlfriends, make not a jot of difference ...

"I didn't ask for these eyebrows. They just sort of appeared. I shaved them off once when I was about 10 and they grew back sort of crooked and weird."
Christian Slater

"I've got a very big butt."
Jean Claude van Damme

"I look dorky in all my films. Mine is not a pretty face."
Harrison Ford

"Early on in my career, I remember casting directors taking one look at me and saying, 'We're looking for someone handsome.' Not that I think I'm great looking but that really hurt."
Kevin Costner

And you'd think the man who got Kim Basinger to the altar wouldn't have another wish in the world ...

"I get up every morning and all I think about is

what's wrong. I'd like to have a nose job – and I wish
I could lose six or seven pounds."
Alex Baldwin

Film stars and sportsmen are paid to look good.
A lot of their success is down to how their body
functions and appears. It's pointless to compete
because their access to professional help is
unlimited. There is a greater emphasis on training
for films than ever before. Perfect pectorals and
bulging biceps don't come naturally or easily –

personal trainers and dieticians are behind every glistening bulge. Refashioning your body to such extremes can be done, but you have to be a fanatic.

GET REAL

But there are realistic changes that you can make, and the key to unlocking this new you is faith; faith in that mass of masculinity at your disposal – namely your body and your mind. OK, there are going to be some things that you can't change ... for instance, your height, your body frame, and the colour of your skin. Basic things like these are not worth getting hung up about, so make an agreement with yourself now to learn to love and be proud of them.

The first step to making any changes to your appearance is to take a good, long look at yourself. How long has it been since you looked at your body naked? You probably spend hours gazing at the thing covered up, but hardly a moment examining the whole raw state.

Looking at yourself in the nude before a full-length, truth-telling, light-of-day mirror can be uncomfortable. But the experience will tell you an awful lot more about your body and how you feel about it.

Start by acknowledging the body bits with which

you have no problem. Look in the mirror and say, 'I have strong hands', or 'My face is a good shape and I like the colour of my hair.' Then progress on to the body features you're less happy with. Look at your chest and say, 'OK, it's smaller than I'd like, but I can live with it.' The truth is, once you accept yourself, you'll feel better about yourself – and you will look better.

You know, in your heart of hearts, that a little attitude goes a lot further than a tiny, tight bum and a perfectly chiselled jaw. Make your body your friend. Your body is just one small part of who you are, so don't treat it like your greatest enemy.

AIM FOR THE TOP SCORE

Women's magazines over the years have done countless surveys on what women look for in a man and not once has physical perfection achieved the top score. When it comes to what makes a man attractive, a decent personality and sense of humour will always get higher results.

Boys should count themselves lucky, as girls are not let off the hook so easily. There is far more media and social pressure for a girl to look drop-dead gorgeous than for a guy. And many girls get frustrated with the strain of it all. Don't fall into that trap.

And remember, just concentrating on your image and ignoring the other things that make you who your are, like your brains, your personality and so on, is really a pretty limiting experience. The bottom line is learning to feel comfortable with yourself. Good looking is just as much about state of mind as it is about the state of your body. Once your self-confidence is strong, you'll be able to accept the way you look. Honestly.

Chapter Two

FACING THE FACTS (SPOTS AND ALL)

There is an awful lot of nonsense written and talked about skin care. But similarly, there is masses of extremely simple, sound advice that often gets ignored.

It would be wonderful to be able to explain the secret of how to achieve perfect skin and how to keep it perfect all the time. But the truth is, no matter how well it's looked after, your skin will normally cause you plenty of problems during your teens.

This is due to the enormous number of hormones you're producing – which tend to be over-active during your teens but will calm down in a few years. These hormones stimulate your skin glands to produce more oil (sebum), which is what encourages spots.

These hormones may sound like nothing but trouble but they aren't all bad – they're extremely useful and necessary for your bone growth and sexual maturity. It might seem unfair and hideous at the time, but it's an inevitable part of growing up. Besides, there are many ways of reducing the stress and embarrassment caused by skin problems – fast.

THICK SKINNED

Boys' skin is about 24 per cent thicker than girls', and is generally firmer and stronger too, but it is prone to the same irritations – spots and blemishes.

The skin on your face needs special care. It's more delicate than the skin on the rest of your body – which spends most of its time carefully covered up out of harm's way. The skin on your face has its work cut out – being bombarded with anything from strong sunshine to bracing winds and rain. Grimy dirt and germs all take their toll too. Your face has a tough job battling with the elements and pollution every day, so the least you can do in return is to try to look after it!

SO WHAT'S YOUR TYPE?

Most skin falls into one of three categories, depending on how much or how little sebum is produced.

Desert Dry

Dry skin doesn't contain enough sebum. It's particularly sensitive to the sun and and can be irritated easily by soap. It often feels tight and flaky. Extremely dry skin is often very sensitive and sore – it's a bit like having chapped lips, but all over your face. It's quite rare for teenagers to suffer from excessively dry skin.

Oily Boily

Oily skin produces too much sebum. It looks shiny and feels greasy soon after washing. The bad news is that dirt and grime are most attracted to this type of skin so you're more likely to get spots and blackheads. But the good news is that oily skin has the last laugh later in life. Once your hormones have calmed down and your glands have stopped producing so much oil, you are left with a healthy, glowing complexion. Oily skin is also less likely to get wrinkles later on so it gives you a youthful-looking face for longer.

A Stunning Combo

Combination skin is the most common skin type, and it's what it sounds like – a combination of both oily and dry skin. The oiliest area is the panel along the central part of the forehead, down the nose and over the chin, making a 'T' shape. The rest of the skin on the face is dryish. It sounds complicated, but it is, in fact, no more of a problem than the others.

Normal

Normal skin is much like combination skin but the differences between the oily and dry areas are much less noticeable. Normal skin needs just as much care, as there might be days when it feels prone to being slightly oily or dry.

If you've got great skin all the time, then you're one of the few lucky ones. But if you're like the rest of us and you've got skin that's prone to developing spots, it's that much more difficult to keep it looking perfect. But with proper care there's no reason why you can't still look healthy and handsome.

COMING CLEAN

Call them spots, zits or acne, they're all the same thing. But having spots doesn't mean you're dirty. When your skin starts to break out in spots, it's very rarely to do with a lack of cleaning – in fact most people with skin problems tend to fall into the trap of over-washing, which makes their skin dry and flaky. Your skin can be irritated by harsh or abrasive cleaning products, so you need to use and choose what you put on your face carefully –

without being conned.

SENSITIVE SOUL

Sensitivity has become the latest buzzword in the skin care industry. Almost every major manufacturer now includes special products aimed at people with over-sensitive skin. It follows other successful trends like diet drinks and preservative-free food. But sensitivity could be a marketing gimmick to make you buy new products.

It's very difficult to suss out if you need special 'sensitive' products or not, as there is no way of judging everyone's idea of sensitivity. That uncomfortable, tight, taut feeling you might describe as a sensitive allergy, others might simply dismiss as dryness and slap on more moisturiser.

Research has shown that 70 per cent of the population consider themselves to have sensitive skin. This is usually after one bad experience with a skin care product. But skin care professionals feel it's probably more likely to be only three to five per cent of people who actually suffer an allergic bad reaction.

If you are convinced that your skin is sensitive, simplicity is the best approach. Go for products that list water as their main ingredient. And while reading the label, don't immediately believe any of their exotic claims. Fragrance-free and unscented aren't the same thing. An 'unscented' product may contain fragrances that block each other out, meaning your nose won't react to them – but your skin might.

If you are worried about a bad reaction to any facial products, test them on your body first. Apply a five pence-size blob on your inner arm, then cover it with a sticking plaster for two days. If your skin is red, itchy or dry after 48 hours, then you're probably allergic to the product. But make sure you're not allergic to sticking plasters first or the results will be very misleading!

GO EASY ON THE GOO

You may have heard your mum, sister or girlfriend going on about having to cleanse, tone and moisturise as part of their beauty routine, witnessed an alarming amount of bottles and discarded cotton wool once they've finally vacated the bathroom, and wondered what all the fuss was about. Well, you were right – it is all a load of fuss, and on the whole, a waste of time and money. Quite simply, the more lotions and potions the manufacturers make you think you need, the more you'll end up buying.

The only products you really need are a cleanser and occasionally a moisturiser – unless you've got

really dry skin, in which case it will need
moisturising every day. Toners are optional – their
job is to refresh and rebalance your skin, but if your
cleanser's good enough you won't need them.

CLEANSER v SOAP

If the sensation of splashing cool water on your face
when washing with soap makes you feel clean and
refreshed, look for a gentle, splash-off cleanser
instead – often called a 'facial wash'. There are lots
to choose from and they are ideal for combination
or normal skins. There is nothing really wrong with
most soaps, but you might find they wash off too
much of your skin's natural oils, leaving a tight
feeling. For your face and neck, a more gentle
product makes more sense. Cleansers shouldn't
leave your skin feeling dry or irritate spots.

If you've got oily skin, it's very tempting to use a
strong cleanser to strip off the excess oil – but don't.
Your skin will only react to the harshness by
producing more oil. It sounds topsy-turvy, but oily
skins would do better with a gentle oil-based
cleanser which can actually limit oil production and
leave your skin supple – not greasy. For a dry skin,
use a creamy cleanser that can be wiped off with
tissue or rinsed off, and follow it with a rich
moisturiser.

MYTHS ABOUT MOISTURISERS

Not everyone needs to use moisturisers all the time. Normal and oily skins produce enough lubrication to keep feeling soft and flexible. After certain events, like a hot shower or a day in the sun, you may need to add extra moisture – but not every single time.

As you get older and reach your mid-twenties, your oil glands become less active – this is when you'll start to need to use a moisturiser regularly to maintain a good balance. Meanwhile, look for a lightweight moisturiser that contains a UV sunlight protector.

PAYING MORE? WHAT FOR?

There isn't much difference between cheap and expensive skin care products. A lot of it is down to the packaging and name, and obviously if something is in a flash bottle you should expect to pay more for it. For instance, a pump-action cleanser is going to cost more than one in a squeezy tube or bottle, as you are paying for all the moving parts.

Usually the first place to look for a decent cleanser or moisturiser is by the basin at home! Skin type often runs in the family, so see what your mum or sister uses. Take the chance to test a variety of products, so you can get to know which you prefer.

THE LOWDOWN ON SCRUBBING UP

Body and facial scrubs (also known as exfoliating creams) have become big business, but most skin care specialists remain sceptical about them.

The idea is that the small grains in exfoliating products scrub off the dead skin cells which sit on your skin's surface, making it look dull. Once the cells have been removed, your skin appears brighter and smoother, and feels invigorated and fresh.

However, your skin is a finely-balanced organ which has been continually growing and shedding its dead outer layer all by itself all your life. If you start scrubbing off that top layer, you're not doing it any favours because you need that layer to protect your face from sun exposure and infections. It's also thought that facial scrubs are too gritty and can cause microscopic tears on delicate facial skin.

Scrubs are great if you feel that your skin looks sluggish and you actually have rough, dry patches that you want to get rid of. But the best advice is to save scrubs for use from the shoulders down, where your skin is thicker and will benefit from the massage.

BOYS' OWN

Male skin care is a multi-million pound business and one of the fastest growing in the industry, so most major chemists now stock skin care ranges that are specifically aimed at men and boys.

Although what's inside is not that different to what females use, you might prefer the perfume and packaging. Either way, you shouldn't be shy about using or choosing skin care.

"I've got no objection to men using face-packs, cleansers or moisturisers, but I draw the line at

mascara and eye shadow."
Linda Lusardi – former page 3 model

ZITS ARE THE PITS

At least 70 per cent of all teenagers have acne at
one time or another, but the fact that it is so
common doesn't make it any easier to cope with.
Worrying and fretting about spots seems to come
with the territory but it's really worth making an
effort to stop worrying. Acne can be made worse by
all that extra stress.

Acne tends to be worse in boys and affects the
face, shoulders, back and chest most because that's
where hair follicles are in the greatest numbers. The
excess oil – which is typical for a teenage skin – can
gather in the follicles and can turn into blackheads
or whiteheads or become inflamed into angry, pus-
filled spots. But acne usually disappears between
the ages of 16 and 25. Although you cannot prevent
acne from appearing, you can at least treat it.

Blast Out Blackheads and Wipe Out Whiteheads

These are two of the most common skin complaints
and they are nothing to do with dirt – so cleansers
are not going to help. Once again, they are all down
to your skin's over-eager oil production during this

stage in your life. Some people swear by steaming them out, which is done by holding the head, covered by a towel, over a bowl of hot water. It is true that the steam will cause your pores to open but it will also swell the cells that are partly blocked, and could result in a complete blockage and eventually a spot.

There is really only one way to eke out blackheads and whiteheads and that is by physically squeezing them out. But never touch your face unless you have really clean hands and that means under the nails as well. Germs will be only too happy to jump onto your face from your fingers and infect your pores further.

You need to treat blackheads and whiteheads with a lot of respect or you'll end up in even more bother. When squeezing a blackhead there is a danger that you might squeeze the plug of oil deeper into the skin, causing inflammation and possibly more spots and scarring.

Instead, try using a special spoon called a blackhead remover which you can get from the Body Shop. It has a tiny metal handle with a spoon shape on one end with a hole in it. You place the hole over the blackhead, squeeze down and the plug pops out. Smooth antiseptic cream over it to finish.

X Marks the Spot

When your mum says 'Don't touch your spots,' she

might as well be saying 'Pick at them until your heart's content,' because everyone finds fiddling with the fascinating lumps and bumps on their face irresistible. The trick is to know when to touch them and when to leave well alone.

Never squeeze a spot unless it's really ready to rupture. Only once the spot has a ripe white head on it can you gently press down either side, to get out the offending pus. Don't get so enthusiastic that the whole thing starts to bleed and flare up. Instead, at the first sight of blood, wash your hands, clean the spot with mild antiseptic and let it get on with healing naturally. This way you'll avoid scarring or driving the spot deeper into your skin.

Three Steps to Heaven – and Fewer Spots

1) If your spots are not too frequent and widespread you can try a spot treatment from the chemist. Spot creams which contain the chemical benzoyl peroxide can be very effective. There are different strengths available and different bases for different skin types, so it's a good idea to ask the pharmacist for their advice on which to use. Fair or sensitive-skinned people should start on the lowest strength but everybody should check which is best for their skin type. Once you have read the blurb, you have to give the product time to work. No product is going to zap zits overnight, so give it at least four weeks before giving up. You might need

to experiment with a few products before you find one that's right for you.

If you are using a spot cream from the chemist containing benzoyl peroxide on your chest, arms or back, it's worth remembering that it can bleach out patches on your clothing. During the day, wear a loose-fitting, old cotton T-shirt or vest under your clothes so your best stuff doesn't get spoilt.

2) If you don't notice any improvement in your spots, it's time to book an appointment with your doctor. Don't think that you're wasting their time – they are there to help! Spots are a serious problem and your doctor understands this and should be sympathetic. If they think it will help your skin, you can get a prescription of antibiotics. Once again, it's going to take time for your treatment to work – and unfortunately many people give up hope. *Don't give up* or you'll never know if your spots would have got better.

3) If you're still suffering, your next option is to see a skin care specialist called a dermatologist. They can prescribe a wider range of treatments and have up-to-the-minute knowledge of the latest treatments. Your doctor will have to recommend that you see a dermatologist, and sadly the waiting list can be months long, but you are entitled to a second opinion, so don't be put off.

Tricks to Try

Many acne sufferers find that their spots are less frequent during the summer months. The strong UV light from the sun quickly heals inflamed skin, and a tan tends to give a healthy glow and cover any redness. But be extremely careful not to add to the redness by getting sunburned, and always use a sun protection lotion.

Maybe your local sports centre has a sunbed. It's certainly not a great idea to go on sunbeds too often, as it has been proven that they give an ageing and drying effect to your skin very quickly and, used repeatedly, the ultraviolet rays can lead to skin cancer. However, if it's the depths of winter when your spots are giving you serious grief, the artificial sunlight from one sunbed session might help to soothe them.

From the sounds-weird-but-does-work department comes this quick tip from one of the jet-setting supermodels. Take some eye drops, the sort that promise to 'get the red out' of bloodshot eyes by soothing and shrinking inflamed blood vessels. Apply it as a quick fix for small spots and blemishes on the face. It zaps mini-zits into invisibility in no time.

You can disguise spots temporarily by using a special kind of make-up called concealer. It's tinted to match your skin colour and some brands are medicated so that they won't aggravate your spots.

It often comes in a twisty tube that looks like a lipstick. Concealers can be very greasy, which means by the time you get through the school gates it's already smudged off.

Try applying a thin layer of concealer, and then dust down with a little talc on a tissue. It should stop the concealer shifting off your face. Concealer actually covers your pores, so it's important that you wash it off thoroughly at night.

Feeding Your Face from the Inside

There is no proof that crisps, chocolate and other fatty foods make your spots worse. The excess oil you produce in your skin has nothing to do with your diet. BUT, before you drop this book and race to your local newsagent, your skin does reflect what's going on inside.

If you eat loads of junk food – which is low in vitamins and roughage – and you're not getting enough sleep or fresh air, your skin will look bad. Pasty, sallow skin that's lacking in life is not very attractive. So as a general rule, looking after your skin, diet and overall health are the same thing. Sorry!

Nice 'n' Natural

Clothes made of natural fibres like cotton or pure wool will let your sweat escape much more easily, which is better for your skin. Spots just love synthetic fabrics like 100 per cent polyester or nylon that don't let your skin breathe and trap stale sweat. Exercise is extremely important, but it does make you sweat that much more, so if your spots are bad on your shoulders and back, avoid all synthetic sports clothing.

Living with Your Acne – It Can Happen!

Peering at your spots, close up against the mirror, under the harsh bathroom striplight, gives the impression that yours must be the worst skin in the world. But instead of sinking into the depths of despair, take yourself away from it. Give your poor face a break! Your spots need a chance to disappear without you following every inch of their progress. You can still enjoy your life while your treatment takes effect!

There is a well-established self-help group for anyone suffering from acne, called the Acne Support Group. To join and receive a regular newsletter, send a SAE to the Acne Support Group, 16 Dufours Place, Broadwick Street, London W1V 1FE.

Chapter Three

GET READY, GET SET, GET A RAZOR!

A lot of lads are seriously keen to start waving a razor around the bathroom. To many, it's considered macho and a sign of maturity. It can certainly seem unjust when boys younger than you already have some sort of fluff on their face and yours is still as smooth as a baby's bottom. But the fact is, starting to shave is nothing to do with being a 'man'. Your body will develop and do its own thing in its own time, and there is nothing you can do to accelerate this. Besides, once the novelty of shaving for the first few times has worn off, most men find it becomes a real bore. A man has an average of 30,000 whiskers on his face, and will spend up to 3,350 hours (139 days) of his lifetime removing that once-longed-for facial fuzz!

SHAVING BACK THE YEARS

Exactly when men started to shave is not known,

but it is thought that the Egyptians, Greeks and Romans shaved their faces as a sign that they were from noble and wealthy families. And Alexander the Great's soldiers shaved off their beards to avoid them being seized by the enemy during battle!

Shaving has certainly got easier these days. In ancient times the techniques used to remove facial hair were seriously painful. Plucking or singeing with a red-hot iron were both popular, but using a sharpened shell or flint was probably preferable.

With the development of hardened steel, the cut-throat razor came into use and shaving became relatively painless, but it was American salesman Mr King C Gillette who transformed shaving in 1895 with the introduction of his safety razor.

These days the most popular method of shaving is still the traditional wet shave. You might want to dry shave with an electric razor, but to start with, your choice depends on what equipment you get.

WET WET WET SHAVING

Equipment needed: razor with blade, shaving cream, gel or stick, shaving brush, sponge or flannel, warm water, towel, mirror and good lighting!

Shave first thing in the morning when your skin has rested and is therefore at its least sensitive. It's a good idea to shave after a bath or shower, as this softens the skin and opens the pores.

Start by rinsing your brush (if you have one) and razor under very hot water, to ensure that they're clean. Then gently massage the skin with a mild cleanser and warm water, followed by a thorough rinsing.

Cover the area to be shaved with shaving foam or cream. If you're using a shaving stick, whip up a good lather with a shaving brush first.

Start shaving the softer areas like the lower cheek first to give extra time for hairs on coarser areas like the upper lip and chin to soften. Pull the skin gently downwards to stretch it, and make short strokes in the direction of the hair growth with the razor. Rinse the blade every few strokes to remove the foam and hairs clogging the blade.

It is possible to shave upwards in the opposite direction to your hair growth but most men find it unnecessarily difficult and there is more chance of nicking the skin. However, if you take extra care, it does give a closer shave.

When you have finished, rinse your face thoroughly with plenty of cool water to close the pores and freshen the skin.

The Close Shave

When you shave regularly it's a good idea to change the razor-blade every third shave, as they go blunt very quickly. A blunt razor won't give you a close shave and can leave your face sore from all that extra scraping. It's also more hygienic, as inflammation of the beard area may be caused by bacteria on a used blade. This also means you should never share or lend your razor to anyone else.

ELECTRIC DREAM

Equipment needed: electric razor, either battery operated or with a lead for mains electricity.

An electric razor reduces the chance of skin irritations which can be caused by wet shaving. It is important that your skin is completely dry before starting to shave or the electric razor will feel like it's dragging on the skin. Your skin must still be clean, so wash with a gentle cleanser and pat dry thoroughly.

Switch the razor on, and run it over your face. Be firm, but don't press too hard. When finished, you will need to clean the hair from inside the razor each time you use it. A small brush is normally provided for this.

HOW OFTEN?

How often you shave is totally personal to you.
However, when you first start there is no need to get
over-zealous! Give your upper lip or chin a chance
to get used to having a piece of sharp metal being
scraped over it every day. If it feels in the least bit
tender, take care and leave well alone for a few
days. Let your skin have a chance to repair itself
naturally.

DOUBLE BENEFITS

Shaving soon gets boring but it's extremely good
exercise for your face! All that grimacing and
twisting is like a daily aerobics class for the jaw. It
can help keep a double chin at bay and leaves a
really smooth, tingly-fresh face.

THE CUTTING EDGE

Supermodel time-saver: if you nick your skin when
shaving, hold a used tea bag over the cut. The
tannin in the tea will stop the blood flow in
minutes.

AFTERSHAVE?

As shaving removes the top layer of dead skin cells, it can leave your face a little dry and red, so this is when you'd expect to use, as the word implies, an aftershave. But don't even think about it! You'd do a lot better in the long run to use a soothing moisturiser.

Harsh alcohol-based aftershaves will only irritate the skin further and in time will have quite a dramatic premature ageing and drying effect on your face – which is not desirable!

If it's the scent you're after, wait a while to give your skin a chance to settle after shaving. If you're in a hurry, try an aftershave balm instead, which is a moisturiser-based lotion which is nowhere near as strong on the face after shaving.

AND AFTER THE AFTERSHAVE

Male fragrance sales are soaring and the modern man is no longer relying on birthdays and Christmases to replenish his stocks. So there is nothing to stop you from testing out a few scents yourself; after all, you're going to wear it so you've got to like it.

Male fragrances come in three strengths: aftershave, cologne and the most powerful – eau de toilette. A classic mistake a lot of boys make is to splash it all over liberally in the hope that the more they use, the more attractive they will be. Smelling good is attractive to girls but it's not a sure-fire way to get a girlfriend, and overdoing it could have the opposite effect.

Even the mildest aftershave has a lasting effect and therefore should be used sparingly. Boys tend not to own masses of different brands of aftershave, so if you only have one or possibly two favourites, your nose quickly becomes accustomed to the smell and unaware of its strength, which is another reason you might use too much.

And remember: heat expands fragrance, making it stronger still – so in the summer use aftershaves particularly sparingly.

SCENT PACKING

Spending large sums of money on scent is not going to buy you instant sex-appeal. Fragrance advertisers try to lure you in cleverly by showing what they think are successful and attractive men with flashy lifestyles using their scent. Cheaper colognes can be equally as good, but since a sense of smell is so personal you will only be able to tell what you like by trying it out.

If the one you like is too expensive, ask for it as a gift, instead of relying on what your mum, aunty or girlfriend chooses for you. Aftershaves, when used sensibly, do last a long time – so they're not such bad value. But don't forget to use it altogether, as the smell can go off or it can evaporate if left open and then it really is a waste of money. However, most aftershaves are designed to last between two and four years before spoiling.

Advice: if there's still aftershave in the bottle after four or five years, next time, buy a smaller bottle. But remember: owning or using aftershave is not essential.

Chapter Four

SAY CHEESE

Your mouth is one of the busiest parts of your body. Apart from the obvious eating and drinking it is also your most useful asset when you want to express yourself – by talking, smiling, laughing and kissing.

Having good teeth is half the battle towards having good looks. Being sure about your smile is the most instant way of making yourself more attractive. Next time you're watching TV, take a close look at the radiant-white smiles of most young actors. These days, many entertainers have cosmetic dentistry to improve their career prospects. You don't need to have all this flashy surgery to have good-looking teeth. Anyway, slightly yellowish teeth are actually healthier than pure white ones.

NEW AND IMPROVED

Since the widespread introduction of fluoride

toothpastes in the early 1970s, levels of tooth decay have dropped dramatically. Back in 1968, the average teenager had just under ten fillings; this statistic has now fallen to nearly half that. Bad news for the dentist you might think – but you'd be wrong. Although drilling and filling aren't quite as common, dentists have their work cut out with a whole new range of cosmetic dentistry services that you can benefit from.

Straightening, capping, crowning, whitening, cleaning, polishing and veneering are all tricks of the dental trade that will help you smile with confidence. Remember, your dentist is someone who is there to help you keep your teeth – and your looks. If you think your smile could be improved by a brace or an overall polish and check-up, you need to talk to your dentist. Soon.

NO EXCUSES

Check-ups and most courses of treatment from your NHS dentist are free until you are 18 and while you are a student.

PLAQUE ATTACK

Neglect your teeth and they'll soon start to look

nasty. Worse still, they'll start to give you a lot of grief in the way of agonising pain. Bad breath and other unpleasant oral odours are normally a direct result of uncared-for teeth.

Any particles of food left on your teeth will encourage bacteria. In no time at all a thin film of this bacteria – called plaque – will coat your teeth. (You can feel a furry texture with your tongue.) Plaque in itself is not harmful, it's how long it is left to build up that's important.

Gum infections have always been the most common cause of tooth loss, and it's the bacteria in plaque that causes gum disease. The first sign is that your gums bleed when they are brushed. Whatever anyone tells you, it is not natural for your gums to bleed – even if it doesn't hurt. In the end, the gum may become destroyed, causing your teeth to fall out, and that will be the end of that. Healthy gums are pink and moist. If your gums look red and swollen, it means you should see your dentist.

TOOTH DECAY AND THE SUGAR GANGS

Sugar is the number one bad guy here. Sugar gangs up with the bacteria in your mouth to make an acid. This acid first attacks the tooth enamel and then burrows deeper until it reaches the sensitive nerve. That's when you'll know all about it – ouch!

Eating sweets and having fizzy drinks between meals is how most of the damage is done. If you have a weakness for these snacks, try to eat them straight after meals instead, as your saliva will have had a chance to build up. Your saliva, which is slightly alkaline, will neutralise the acid and your teeth can once again breathe a sigh of relief. Anything that increases the flow of saliva and speeds up this process should help reduce tooth decay, so you could occasionally chew a sugar-free gum.

TONGUE LASHING

The majority of oral bacteria lives not on your teeth but on your tongue. Our great-grandads were better clued-up than we are about this – in the 1907 *Army and Navy Stores* catalogue they advertised tortoiseshell tongue scrapers at nine shillings each. Researchers now say that regular brushing of your tongue with your toothbrush is a very effective way of reducing the build-up of plaque and preventing bad breath.

TWICE A DAY

Get into the habit of brushing your teeth twice a

day, once in the morning and last thing at night. Take care to brush all three surfaces of your teeth – the back, front and biting surfaces. Brush downwards for your top teeth and upwards on the lower teeth, away from the gums. Use small circular movements on the biting surfaces.

CHOOSING A BRUSH

Manual
Your toothbrush should have a long, narrow neck to give easy access to all areas of the mouth; some people find that an angled neck on the brush helps with the back teeth. The brush should also have a comfortable handle and a rounded head.

Shock-absorbing Toothbrushes
These are the latest design to be found at the chemist's counter. They are designed to prevent excessive pressure on the teeth and gums during brushing. They have a wavy plastic spring on the handle just below the head of the toothbrush. It's hard to tell how effective they are, but if it's what you fancy and you can afford the few extra pence, it won't do you any harm.

Electric
There are only a few brands on the market, and

they come well recommended. When choosing an electric toothbrush, check it features a back-and-forth action and rechargeable batteries. If you're a bit of a gadget fan and think an electric toothbrush will encourage regular brushing – it might be the answer!

Whichever toothbrush you choose, remember to change it every eight to 12 weeks for continued effective brushing.

WHICH PASTE?

A fluoride toothpaste, of course! Fluoride is a natural substance that protects your tooth enamel, making teeth stronger and less likely to decay. Look for brands that carry a seal of approval from the British Dental Health Association (BDHA or BDA). But remember, a toothpaste is only as good as your brushing, so brush up on your technique for best results.

TO FLOSS OR NOT TO FLOSS?

Yes, yes, yes! Dentists are forever singing the virtues of dental floss and that's because it does do a very good job. It's a bit tricky to get the hang of, but your mouth really does feel fresh and snoggable after some effective flossing! You can buy waxed or unwaxed dental floss. Wax tends to slip between the teeth more easily if your teeth are packed tightly together, but basically, choose whichever one you like the sound of.

To floss, wrap a length of about 40 cm of the tape around each index or middle finger. Guide the floss through the gap between two teeth and pull it gently up and down, back and forth. This dislodges food particles that may be stuck and cleans the tricky-to-reach area around the gum line.

ANTI-PLAQUE RINSES

There are a number of rinses on the market that claim to reduce the dreaded plaque. Some dentists remain unconvinced, while others have reported positive results. However, none as yet have received the BDA stamp of approval.

CAN YOU DETECT YOUR OWN BAD BREATH?

Short of asking a friend, no, not really. But taste and smell are closely linked. If a meal leaves a strong taste in your mouth, the chances are it'll leave a smell too. Bad breath is usually caused by the build-up of bacteria in the difficult-to-get-at gaps between your teeth. Try smelling your dental floss instead; if it has a strong smell, so will your breath.

Nobody on earth could actually enjoy another person's bad breath. However witty and intelligent your conversation may be, the chances of getting intimate with the girl you fancy will be reduced to a minimum if your breath isn't fresh. So having regular dental check-ups and brushing and flossing your teeth does have big pay-offs.

Chapter Five

EYES RIGHT

Human eyes have been described as the 'windows of the soul' because they are so expressive and reveal many emotions even if you try and keep your feelings hidden. Couples often say that it was their boyfriend's or girlfriend's eyes that attracted them to each other first, and this is why many girls go in for elaborate 'window-dressing' in the form of alluring eye make-up.

In this respect, boys are much more open, as they leave their eyes to speak naturally for themselves. This is a much better option, as your eyes are two of the most delicate organs in your body and all that gloopy mascara and flaky eye-shadow can really irritate them no end.

TIRED-LOOKING EYES

If you watch TV or play on a small-screen computer game hour after hour, your eyes can start to feel gritty or scratchy and might ache. Staring at a flickering screen only a few feet in front of you is forcing your eyes to focus on one particular depth of vision for an unnaturally long length of time. The extra strain you are putting on your eyes makes them tired or sore and can give you dark rings and bags under your eyes.

Dark rings can usually be cured by getting a good night's sleep and by avoiding smoky or polluted atmospheres. As your eyes reflect your general health, they can also develop dark circles from stress or a poor diet. If you've had an injury, all that extra suffering and pain can lead to temporary rings round the eyes. Try to avoid touching and rubbing your eyes as much as possible and after washing your face, quickly splash the eye area with water as cold as you can bear for a few seconds to reduce any irritation or redness.

But if you know that you're getting enough rest and you still seem to have dark panda eyes, then it's probably hereditary. Look at your mum or dad – the chances are that they also have the same sort of colouring around the eyes. If you haven't even noticed the way it looks on them, it probably doesn't look that terrible on you!

People who have darker pigment around the eyes often feel less self-conscious during the summer when their face has a light tan. Everyone feels pasty in the winter anyway, but you could occasionally

try a very subtle facial fake tan to lift your spirits –
see Chapter Seven on sun care.

PUFFINESS

If you've let yourself get over-tired, or you're in the
throes of a bad head cold, hay fever or another
allergy, it's likely your eyes will get puffy and
tender. You can cool the soreness with a gentle
soothing gel, specially formulated for the delicate
eye area – the chemist will know what you mean.
There are several brands available. This will help
your eyes feel more refreshed.

Relaxing back with a couple of slices of chilled
cucumber over the eyes has long been claimed to
alleviate puffiness. It may feel good, but the actual
remedy backfires because when you lie down your
face naturally swells. Instead, try wrapping an ice
cube in a couple of sheets of kitchen towel and
gently dab, not drag, the delicate eye area with the
cool cube for a couple of minutes.

BLOODSHOT EYES

Just as grimy, stained teeth are a real turn-off, so
are bloodshot eyes. The whites of your eyes look
red and veiny and generally make your face look

unhealthy. It's not at all uncommon to suffer occasionally from bloodshot eyes, especially if you're tired or have been in the company of several smokers. It doesn't usually mean there is anything seriously wrong, but if it doesn't clear up quickly you should see a doctor.

There are plenty of eye drop solutions you can buy which 'whiten' your eyes by constricting the tiny blood vessels which run underneath the surface of the eyeball and inner eyelid. These drops have an instant effect and are an ideal cure for bloodshot eyes but they do prevent oxygen reaching the eye's surface and will damage your eyes if you use them too frequently.

EMBARRASSED BY LIGHT LASHES

If you're lucky enough to be a natural blond or red-head, enjoy your special colouring, as the vast majority of people in Britain have mousey mid-brown hair. The one drawback of having a very fair complexion can be pale eyelashes that look nearly non-existent. Larger chemists and department stores sell eyelash dye kits which will give more emphasis to your eyelashes.

Dyeing your lashes sounds a very girlie thing to do, but in fact it's quite common amongst male models, and most lash dyeing kits say that they are for boys too. The effect is nothing like wearing mascara, as it doesn't thicken or lengthen the lashes; it will simply enhance and darken your natural colour and will grow out or fade naturally. But before putting any chemical near your eyes, read the instructions very carefully.

TEST THOSE PEEPERS

It's best to have your vision tested by an optician every couple of years – even if you don't wear glasses at the moment. The test will show up any problems you might have before they get too serious. About one in five teenagers needs glasses. The optician will ask you to take tests for long sight, short sight, colour-blindness and your ability to focus. If you do find you have problems, wearing glasses or contact lenses is the answer.

GETTING TO GRIPS WITH GLASSES

Twenty-five years ago the choice was simple. If you were under 30 you were given small oval frames in either pink, blue or black. Buying good-looking glasses was a hopeless task and having to wear them usually resulted in devastating effects on both your looks and social life. Today, the opposite is true.

Any number of styles are available and many people buy eyewear to flatter their face even if they don't need glasses to help them see!

Fit the Face to the Frames

Begin your search for the perfect frames by looking for a contrasting shape to your face. For instance, if your face is round, round frames will make it seem even more round and most likely, heavier. Next, consider the size of your face. A round face is usually short and fairly wide. It would need a frame shape that is more wide than deep, making the face appear longer and narrower.

To determine your face shape and size, pull your hair back and mentally outline the shape of your face in the mirror. Many boys have a well-defined jawline, which is a bonus as it means the glasses will create a good facial balance.

A square face is often short and wide and flat across the cheeks. The jawline is a definite square shape. Again, this shape should not be repeated in the frame. Look at larger, oval frames that are more wide than they are deep.

An oblong face needs to be shortened, as it is longer than it is wide. Try on frames that have more depth than width in either square or round styles.

A diamond shaped face often has wonderful high cheekbones and is narrower at the eyeline and jawline. A frame with a line on top and a clear bottom would not hide the cheekbones but would add width.

An oval face can take nearly all styles and shapes. But an oval face and oval glasses would be a bit boring, so try on some more angular styles.

Eyebrow Effect

The most natural-looking glasses are ones than don't create a second browline on your face. Notice your facial expressions in the mirror and see how much your eyebrows move and give extra emphasis to what you are saying. If your brow has a soft natural arch, choose a frame that follows its line or just sits a touch above it for an open and aware look.

WRONG

RIGHT

The Round Face

The Square Face

The Oblong Face

The Diamond Face

If your eyebrows aren't a matching pair, or they meet in the middle or grow in an odd shape that you're not happy with – you could try plucking them back into line. Wash your face with hottish water to gently open the pores. Pat your face dry and pluck individual eyebrow hairs from underneath the arch of the brow only. Never remove hairs from above, as this will quickly give you a wobbly and unnatural line, which can take quite a while to grow back.

Glasses for a Lifetime ...

It's a common joke that people sit on their glasses, but some lightweight frames can be extremely fragile and expensive to replace. If you think your glasses are going to have to take a bit of knocking about, choose a pair that are strong so they will survive rough treatment.

Before you settle for the most outrageous frames in the shop, remember that most of the time you might be wearing them with your school uniform. Your new glasses have to look all right with these clothes as well as your weekend gear.

Don't let anyone rush you into buying glasses, and make sure it's your choice and not theirs. Your glasses are personal to you and only you can tell if they meet all your requirements, but having an honest second opinion can be a great help.

THE OTHER OPTION – CONTACT LENSES

Wearing glasses to a sports or dance club can easily result in a disaster – even though most lenses are now shatter-proof, the frames can still break easily. If you are mad keen on these activities, contact lenses could be for you. But that's not to say deliberately break your glasses so you have to be bought contact lenses – your glasses will always be your essential standby even if you are lucky enough to have contact lenses as well.

There are two main types of contact lenses, soft lenses and rigid or hard lenses. Your optician will help you decide which type of lens is best for you, so be sure to tell them about your regular sports or social activities. There is a chance that you might not be able to wear contact lenses: bad eyesight cannot always be corrected by contact lenses; and if your eyes are really sensitive, you might not be able to wear them either.

Soft Lenses

This type of lens is soft and pliable because it contains water. If a soft lens is left out of its storage solution in the open air, it will soon dry up, become brittle and will be ruined for future wearing. When you are wearing soft lenses the liquid in your eyes keeps them moist and will prevent them from drying out. Soft lenses can tear easily and need to be handled with lots of care, but most people find them instantly comfortable from the first day of wearing them. Also, if you are prone to eye infections or allergies, these are the best type for you.

Hard Lenses

Most rigid lenses look and feel like they are made of perspex. They are smaller than soft lenses and are often called 'gas permeable lenses' because they allow essential oxygen to get to and from your eye. They won't tear or shrivel up in the open air, but need just as much care as soft lenses when you're not wearing them. At first, hard lenses are not as comfortable as soft lenses, but they are more hard-wearing and once you get used to them you again won't know they're there.

When you are fitted for your lenses the optician should go through everything you need to know about wearing contact lenses and caring for them. It is important that you understand and follow their advice carefully, as your eyes are very precious.

Chapter Six

THE HAPPY HAIR GUIDE

Hair products have become so sophisticated and the jargon so scientific that the blurb on a bottle of shampoo reads more like an extract from a manual about the workings of an internal combustion engine rather than a simple cleaning fluid for dirty hair.

What it boils down to is the same old story: the more products the manufacturers make you think you need, the more you'll buy. But having said that, hair is one area you really can have a lot of fun experimenting with. Trying a dab of this and a squirt of that certainly won't do you any harm. It doesn't have to take a lot of time – you can be lazy about your hair and still have a great-looking style.

THE CUT

There are no Ten Commandments about getting a haircut, but there are guidelines. If you are shorter than some of the other lads, you probably shouldn't have flowing locks or a big bouffant hair style. Trim, shorter styles will keep the balance right. The same goes if you are exceptionally tall: a skinhead haircut can make a tall boy look like a pinhead. Longer hair can look brilliant if you are well-built, but narrow or small shoulders can virtually disappear under long hair.

What to Ask

At some point in every lad's life you get a haircut-from-hell. Having a tragic haircut makes you feel like cutting two eye-holes out of a paper bag and wearing it over your head for at least a week.

So before submitting to the mercy of a stranger wielding sharp scissors, be sure to ask some questions.

Discuss the length first. Lots of hairdressers are accused of being too scissor-happy and taking off more than is required. If you only want an inch off, make sure their idea of an inch is the same as yours. It's often difficult to explain which bits you want short and which bits you want to keep long – so it helps to show the cutter a picture from a magazine to guide them.

Some hairstylists say having a picture can be unrealistic, as the client is disappointed with their new cut because they still don't look like Tom Cruise afterwards. If your hair is a different type or texture to the one in the picture there is no way it'll cut and style the same way. When you do get a haircut you're really happy with, have a photo taken of yourself and show this to the hairdresser – then they can get a really good idea of what effect you are after.

When to Trim

Generally, the experts recommend that you troop back to the salon for a trim every six to eight weeks, but this varies from cut to cut and person to person. When your fringe is blinding you, it obviously needs a prune. If you go back to the same hairstylist, some will trim the fringe for free – if that's all you want doing. Check with them before you leave the salon after you've had a proper cut.

A one-length style requires the least maintenance but a very short cut can start to look shaggy in as little as four weeks. Long layers have a habit of hanging like Dumbo ears before the two-month deadline. The best barometer is the reflection in the mirror. When you feel as if you need a cut – you do.

THE PRICE OF A GOOD SHAMPOO

The cost of shampoos can vary enormously, but whether you buy a posh brand or the supermarket's own, both will get your hair clean. The main differences, apart from the price, are the ingredients. Cheap shampoos contain quite strong detergents that can strip your hair and scalp of its natural oils. This is OK if your hair is problem-free, but otherwise choose a mid-priced shampoo that is suitable for the condition of your hair.

WHICH SHAMPOO FOR WHAT HAIR?

Hair doesn't always fit into the advertised dry, normal and oily categories. Oily hair, for instance, probably means you have an oily scalp, but that doesn't normally mean the ends are oily as well. If your hair is like this, choose a shampoo for oily hair, but then use conditioner on the ends only. (See the section on conditioners for more advice.)

Fine Hair

Fine hair that's also greasy needs a shampoo that won't weigh it down, making it look lank and lifeless. New shampoo ranges are now available that are geared to hair texture too. Choose a gentle, frequent wash shampoo that will remove the dirt, but look for products that also aim to increase the hair's volume so it won't look so stringy.

Fine and dry hair can be quite fly-away. Use a rich, moisturising shampoo for dry hair but don't overload your hair with a heavy conditioner as well; choose one for normal hair, otherwise your hair will become too soft and unmanageable. Shampoos for dry hair can be quite heavy and rich so go easy on the amount – especially if your hair is fine.

Coarse or Curly Hair

If your hair is coarse it can go a bit wiry or frizzy if it gets long or dry. When your hair never seems to sit how you'd like it to, it could probably do with a trim or a gentler shampoo that won't strip off the natural oils (sebum). Thick hair can take richer shampoos and the extra moisturiser will help it lie flat. Look for brands especially for coarse or curly hair.

Curly or coarse hair which is also greasy can be harder to detect than greasy straight hair that goes instantly stringy and lank. Dislodge the dirt and grease from your scalp by combing your hair thoroughly before washing it. This will spread the oils throughout your hair and give your shampoo a chance to wash it all away.

Dreaded Dandruff

More than 60 per cent of the population suffer from dandruff from time to time so it's not exactly what you'd call uncommon. Like the skin on the rest of your body, the skin on your scalp is constantly renewing itself and therefore sheds dry, dead cells all over the shoulders of your favourite black sweatshirt. This is quite a normal process that can come and go from time to time. But dandruff can also be triggered by extra stress or a poor diet. Dramatic changes in your body can make the skin on your scalp shed more rapidly – resulting in dandruff.

Start by switching to a gentle, frequent wash shampoo, to avoid stripping the scalp of its natural oils. Then take the time to massage your scalp when you wash your hair, to get a good circulation of blood to the surface of the skin. If the problem still persists you can try a good medicated or anti-dandruff shampoo but they are harsh on your hair so, as soon as the complaint has cleared up, go back to a normal gentle shampoo. Anti-dandruff shampoos provide a temporary solution, but if the dandruff keeps returning you have to try and alleviate the stress or other problems that are behind it.

TWO-IN-ONE SHAMPOO

Shampoo and conditioner all in one does sound convenient but is only really suitable if you have totally problem-free normal hair. Fine hair has a tendency to go limp and greasy hair won't benefit from being bombarded with the extra conditioner added all-over. But if you already use a two-in-one shampoo and you like the way it leaves your hair, there is no reason to stop using it.

LATHERING UP

To clean your hair really efficiently, check it's really wet through before shampooing. Lather up well by massaging with the tips of your fingers all over your scalp. Rinse your hair equally thoroughly, checking that the water is running completely clear before you stop. Most boys prefer a shower – so if you have one at home, choose products with flip caps or nozzles, which are easy to use 'blind'.

How Much to Use

You may be using twice as much shampoo as you actually need. Depending on the length of your hair and where you live, you only need somewhere between a 20 pence and ten pence-size blob. Hard water always takes that bit longer to lather up than soft water, whether it is shampoo or washing-up liquid. You can tell if your water's hard as there is often a build-up of a whitish sediment round the taps or plug-hole.

If you wash your hair daily, one good lather-up is plenty. If you wash your hair less often and your hair contains a build-up of styling products (like gel or mousse), plan to do two lathers with only the tiniest amount of shampoo each time. If you find your hair is squeaky clean after the first application and rinse – stop there.

How Often

There are over 125 million hair washes in the UK every week, so as a nation we obviously value clean hair! Unfortunately, living in a grimy city means your hair will undoubtedly become coated with dirt and dust more quickly than country dwellers'. But natural things like touching your hair a lot or sweating out on the sports field mean your hair will soon get dirty. Basically, wash your hair whenever you think you need it, and for most people this is about two or three times a week.

TOP CONDITION

Conditioner isn't necessary on really short hair, as the scalp's natural oils keep it in condition. On long or medium-length hair (anything over three inches), conditioning the ends becomes more important, especially if you use a hairdryer regularly or your hair is dyed or feels dry, brittle or frizzy.

Once you have rinsed your hair after shampooing, squeeze the excess water out with your hands. Using the same size blob of conditioner as you would of shampoo, rub the conditioner over the palms of your hands and smooth it into your hair, concentrating on the ends. If your hair is shoulder-length or longer or especially thick and curly, comb the conditioner through to the bottom layers using a wide-tooth comb.

Hair conditioners, even ones that claim to be deep and penetrating, work within a matter of minutes. After that, however long you leave it on, it won't make any difference. Because conditioners are thicker and contain moisturising ingredients, fine hair will soon become lanky and heavy if conditioner is used too frequently. Coarse, curly, dry or damaged hair would benefit from conditioning every time.

BLOW BY BLOW

Hair is weakest when it's wet, so blowing hot air directly at soaking wet hair is the quickest way to damage it. Halve drying time by squeezing the water out of your hair and drying it thoroughly with a clean dry towel. On most hairdryers you can change the heat setting – always use it on the lowest heat or the cold air trigger if it has one. Keep moving your head and hairdryer around to avoid overheating and damaging one spot.

For very short hairstyles, try finger-drying. Lift and style while running your fingers through your hair to add shape and volume. When drying slightly longer hair, blow the underneath hair at the back of the neck first. Then work forwards, drying from the roots down, spending as little time as possible on the ends, where your hair is older and so most easily damaged.

STYLING

"I never go out of the house without my hair gel – if it's not in my bag I panic."
Eddie Kidd, motorcycle stunt man

Coaxing hair into some of the amazing styles featured in magazines is the fun bit. Girls are always quick to notice boys who know how to handle their hair. Sadly, we rarely have the hair we want, and people often admire the opposite to their own. Every hair type has its limitations, and some styles are just not possible with the wrong type of hair.

Professional male models have hairstylists on hand for every photo shoot. Models will readily admit that their hair only looked a certain way for about ten minutes before it flopped or went out of shape, as it's all just for the picture.

The main fault that everybody makes when they first start to use a new hair-styling product is using too much. It's easy to think the more you use, the better the effect will be, but in fact the opposite is true. Styling products that aim to lift the hair or add shape and volume will weigh your hair down and make it even more floppy if you use too much. Towel-dry your hair so it's just damp to the touch. This way you can actually see where your hair needs shaping or styling.

Marvellous Mousse

Styling mousse comes in a gas-propellant canister and is best for adding a soft lift to your hair or accentuating curls. It won't leave your hair sticky or tacky and you can create a gentle shape that won't be stiff to the touch. It would be very unlikely that anyone could tell you have used hair mousse, as its effects are very soft and natural-looking – that's why it can be a bit tricky to get the hang of at first. Most manufacturers recommend using a golf-ball size bit of mousse which you can massage into the roots or scrunch into the ends for casual styles that don't look too groomed. For maximum lift on the fringe or crown, style with a hairdryer.

Gloopy Gel

Hair gel comes in a variety of ranges from 'wet look' to 'firm hold' – but the difference in the finished effect is fairly minimal. Choose from a squeezy tube or screw-top tub and add tiny dabs where you need it. For instant fullness and volume, style gelled hair with a hairdryer.

Styling gel maintains a better hold than mousse and can let you create sleek and bold styles. It is more obvious in your hair than mousse, especially 'wet look', and can leave fine hair feeling a little stiff – but it is easily combed out. A floppy fringe could be gelled out of your eyes, or curls could be slicked down for a sleek, groomed appearance. If you have an annoying bit that sticks up behind your ear, a dab of gel will soon smooth it down. Gel is a very versatile product that can be used on damp or dry hair.

Sculpting Lotion

Sculpting lotion is somewhere between mousse and gel. It often comes in an upright squeezy bottle but isn't as thick as hair gel. It's especially good for longer hair as you can use more of it without a sticky build-up. Apply evenly onto towel-dried hair and style with a hairdryer.

Wax Lyrical

Hairdressers love to use wax because once you are confident with using it, it's great for adding texture and shine. It comes in a tub and looks extremely thick and sticky. You can quickly look like a greasy Italian gangster type if you use a lot at once. Use a tiny dab to add definition to short, layered hair or to smooth out curls. Look for brands that are water-soluble and not too scented.

Hold Fast Hairspray

Hairspray is only really good for gently holding a shape once it's been styled. You can't create a new style successfully with just hairspray alone unless you back-brush your hair as well. Back-brushing is suitable for wild and untamed Edward Scissorhands styles. Simply add hairspray onto a lifted section of your hair and then, using a fine-tooth comb, brush your hair in the opposite direction. This is good for the occasional change of image, but regularly back-brushing your hair will quickly wreck it.

COLOUR ME BAD

Dyeing your hair is the quickest way to change your image and that's why most schools won't let you back through the gates if you've coloured your hair. Boys bleaching their hair is seen as rebellious behaviour and not a suitable look for school life.

If you really are desperate to have a go, avoid disaster by trying a temporary colour over the summer holidays. For a one-off special effect you can get spray-on 'crazy colours' like electric blue or pillarbox red which will come out in a couple of washes. For more natural shades, try a sachet of shampoo-in colour which adds a subtle highlight to your hair and only lasts for about six washes.

CURLY OR STRAIGHT?

Having your hair permed is the only way to achieve longed-for curls permanently, and even these will only last between three and five months. Like everything else in fashion and grooming, boys having their hair permed goes in and out of style periodically. Perms can dramatically change the look of your hair, so you have to be prepared in years to come for friends to laugh at old photos of you with your perm!

When adding strong chemicals to your head it's

always best to get a hairdresser to do it – even though it will cost you lots of money. After your hair is washed and cut, it is rolled onto special perm rollers and the perming solution is then applied. The lotion penetrates into the hair shaft and breaks down its structure so it can be reshaped into curls. It is crucial that this process is timed correctly, as over-permed hair will quickly give you Deirdre Barlow curls.

Having your hair relaxed has become a popular way of transforming naturally curly hair, especially the tight curls of many Black people, into straight styles. Once again a chemical solution is added to the hair, which must be carefully timed to the manufacturer's directions or you could damage both your hair and your scalp.

BRUSHES AND COMBS

Choose a brush with soft, rounded bristles and a comb with wide spaces and blunt teeth to avoid damaging your hair or scalp. The very wide-tooth African comb is best for tight, curly hair; try to get a plastic one as wood can splinter and be unhygienic. Brushing or combing your hair helps remove dust and dirt and spreads the oils down from your scalp, keeping the rest of your hair shiny and in good condition.

STYLE BLITZ

The oils and grease from your head soon build up on your brushes and combs so it's important to wash them regularly to avoid transferring all that grime back onto your clean hair. Pour a bit of shampoo onto a nail brush and clean your comb by gently scrubbing off the dirt.

LOSING HAIR

The life-span of an individual hair is about six years and the overall average growth rate is about five inches a year, but for teenagers this can be as much as seven inches.

Teenage boys can boast about 100,000 hairs per head, so to gather a few hairs each time you brush it is no great loss. In fact it's quite normal to lose about 100 hairs a day. The hairs fall out to make room for new hairs to come through. However, if you think you're losing much more than that, it could be that you're brushing too vigorously and pulling them out before they're ready. Styling products like gel or mousse may have made the hairs stick together so when you comb you're pulling more out each time. Comb small sections, starting at the ends to get rid of any tangles. Don't brush your hair when it's wet because this is when it's at its weakest and most vulnerable to being over-stretched and broken.

SPLIT ENDS

The drying elements of the cold, wind, sun and even central heating can make your hair dull and dry, and hairdryers in particular are famously bad for their damaging effects. But all these forms of rough treatment are possible on hair without resulting in really bad split ends if the ends are cut off before they get in a really bad state.

A split end looks exactly like it sounds – the end of the hair is split like a splinter into two or more individual ends. They are not painful or troublesome, they're simply a sign that your hair has got out of condition. No one ever died from a bad case of split ends, but once you've got them the only way to cure them is with a pair of scissors.

Chapter Seven

SUN 'N' SKIN

Anyone who's been living on this planet for the last few years will have noticed the growing concern about the dangers of over-exposing your skin to the sun.

This latest worry is not a fad that will slowly fade like last summer's tan, it is based on hard facts and statistics that are definitely worth taking notice of – now.

SAVING YOUR SKIN

Skin cancer is the second most common form of cancer in Britain and the fastest growing, with the number of people dying from it doubling every ten years. Experts think this huge increase is linked to the amount of time we are exposing our unprotected skin to the sun. More holidays abroad and the continued trend to want to come back with a tan hasn't helped – and the depletion of the ozone layer is a contributing factor.

It seems so unfair that everything we really enjoy has to be bad for us. This is how it might feel at first, but it's seriously important that you know the facts instead of taking ignorant risks. It's much better to understand the dangers of strong sunlight than to burn your skin to a frazzle on the first day of your holiday and spend the rest of your time feeling sore and sulking in the shade.

Skin cancer is caused by over-exposure to ultraviolet light which comes from the sun. It's a disease which mainly affects adults, but the bad news is that sunburn before the age of 15 definitely seems to increase the risk of skin cancer later in life. You may soon forget getting burnt on holiday, but your skin never does. The good news is that skin cancer can be avoided and if detected early, 90 per cent of cases can be treated successfully.

TANNING TRUTHS

Some sunlight is good for your skin – it helps in the production of vitamin D, which activates the calcium needed for growing strong bones, nails and teeth. Being active outdoors is healthy too – all that fresh air makes you feel alive and keeps you in good condition. But there is no such thing as a healthy suntan.

A tan is your body's attempt to defend itself from sunburn and is evidence that you have damaged your skin. Many teenagers are unable to produce enough brown skin pigment (melanin) to protect them from the sun in Britain – let alone the powerful rays on holiday abroad.

FEEL THE BURN

As anyone who has suffered will tell you, getting sunburnt is one of the most miserable feelings in the world. It can make going for a swim, getting dressed or even trying to sleep an impossibly painful experience.

If you have fair or red hair, blue eyes or freckles you have probably already found that you are particularly susceptible to sunburn. Black- or brown-skinned boys will rarely suffer because they are protected by the high level of melanin in their skin. However, dark skins still need protection, especially for the face, as even black skin will suffer the premature ageing effects of strong UV rays.

LEARNING YOUR LOTIONS

Many people mistakenly believe that our sunlight isn't strong enough to cause any skin problems, but lots of people who have never been out of this country still develop skin cancer.

Prevention is far better than cure, so using a sunscreen cream regularly should become a priority – but this is easier said than done. The labelling on sun lotions has become so confusing that you can be forgiven for never quite making it to the chemist's counter. Use this guide to swot up on your SPFs and UV rays so the sun will never get the better of you.

UV – Ultraviolet light is part of the solar spectrum. Its rays can be divided into three wavelengths, two of which are important to screen for skin protection: UVA and UVB.

UVA – Ultraviolet rays which accelerate the drying out, wrinkling and ageing of your skin. Think UVA equals A for ageing – it leads to craggy, super-lined skin when you are older. UVA rays can penetrate through the windows in the classroom or car, so sit in a shady seat whenever possible.

UVB – These are the burning and browning ultraviolet rays and the main cause of skin cancer. Think UVB equals B for burning. The SPF number indicates the UVB protection level of your sun cream.

SPF – Sun Protection Factor. The SPF number is a guide to the time you can spend in the sun. If you can tolerate ten minutes in the sun without burning, then SPF 15 will allow you 15 times ten minutes (150 minutes).

Water-resistant and Waterproof

Water-resistant sunscreens stay on the skin for a minimum of 45 minutes and waterproof products should last for double that time. Swimming trunks and towels can quickly rub off sun creams, so always re-apply after any water sports.

Sun Block

This is a highly concentrated sun protection cream

that should have an SPF of at least 30. It is ideal for lips, noses and tops of ears, but remember to re-apply regularly (about every two hours) as it's easy to rub or sweat off sun block. Your lips contain very little or no pigment at all so they are especially vulnerable to the sun's rays. During the summer carry a lipstick-size sun block to keep your lips kissable.

SUN FACT FILE TO FOLLOW

The only way to be sure of enjoying the summer safely is to prevent over-exposure to the sun's strong rays.

Try to keep out of the sun when it is at its most dangerous – between 11 am and 3 pm. Make maximum use of shady areas like under trees, or take advantage of indoor facilities at this time.

During a really hot spell, either at home or on holiday, wear loose, baggy, close-weave cotton clothes. An oversized T-shirt is perfect and a baseball cap can also provide useful protection – flip it back to front to cover the back of your neck, which is particularly vulnerable to sunburn. Skimpy clothes, like vest tops, reveal too much of your shoulders – which is the commonest area for severe sunburn. Keep them covered whenever possible. Your best choice of T-shirt for a really hot day spent outside would be one in a pale colour. Black clothing absorbs the sun's heat, making you feel hotter, while white reflects the sun's strong rays onto your face and increases your chance of burning, so choose coloured T-shirts in medium-light shades.

Cover exposed parts of your skin with sunscreen. A minimum sun protection factor (SPF) value of 15 which has UVA and UVB screen should be used. It should not be the main method of protection as it's expensive and requires re-application every few hours – combine using sunscreen with the advice above.

Your eyes can also be damaged by excessive sun exposure and should be protected. Look for sunglasses that have a UV (ultraviolet) filter.

With all their glorious weather and beach life, the Australians take skin cancer very seriously. Posters, TV and magazines are constantly urging Aussies to Slip, Slop, Slap – Slip on a shirt, Slop on sunscreen and Slap on a hat. They even have beach police to remind you of the dangers and they'll spray you with sun lotion if you look under-protected!

FAKING IT

If you can't bear the thought of going through the summer without that golden glow, fake tan lotion is the way to go. There was a time when self-tan lotions made you look like the streaky orange Tango man, but in recent years the manufacturers have responded to the demand for a really convincing fake tan cream.

It's nice to know that sometimes the customer gets what the customer wants and you can rest assured that successful bronzing now comes out of a bottle.

Self-tanners come in a wide range of shades from 'light' to 'very dark' – choose a colour that you would realistically go if you were tanning naturally.

To avoid blotches and streaks it will take time and careful application. Have a bath or shower and if you use a body scrub, exfoliate dry areas like knees, elbows and heels – a flannel rubbed over these areas will do just as well. Dry yourself really thoroughly and then lightly moisturise your body and face – especially on dry bits so your skin is ultra-smooth.

Squeeze out a grape-sized blob of cream and rub over the palms of your hands. It's usually white when it first comes out of the bottle and starts to react with your skin and the oxygen in the air after about four hours, much like when you bite into an apple and then leave it and it slowly turns brown. Start massaging it onto your body, taking special care to blend well under the chin and backs of knees. All fake tan creams have a fairly unpleasant chemical smell but it soon goes away and is completely harmless.

If you are using fake tan for the first time on your face, go easy. Look for products specially designed for use on the face. Build up colour gradually rather than attempting deep tan tones overnight.

For realistic results, wipe away some of the cream with a tissue before it starts to work on the insides of your arms, eyebrows, hairline, eyelids and behind your ears – all the areas that tan less naturally and where the cream can collect.

To finish, gently scrub the palms of your hands and under your fingernails with a nail brush to remove all traces of fake tan cream. Brown palms are the biggest giveaway!

Fake tan creams only last about four to five days but if you are really unhappy with the results, a body or face scrub will soon remove every last trace. Wait for the cream to have sunk in a bit before getting dressed as it can stain your clothes, but it should all come out in the wash.

Chapter Eight

YOUR BODY AND OTHER BITS

Baring well-toned bodies in all their glory is what the world of advertising is best at. Pictures of gorgeous girls in glamorous settings have always outnumbered those of men ten to one – but times are changing.

It's no longer such a culture shock to see a super-fit, semi-naked man promoting anything from ice cream to fizzy water. Similarly, on the music scene, never have there been so many all-boy bands wearing so few clothes. This re-awakening of beefcake is enough to send any boy who's a bit unsure about his body into a fit of insecurity. But that's just the reaction the advertisers are hoping to achieve.

Media images are a strong influence and can leave you feeling quite inadequate. Perhaps they can be used as a good reminder that you do feel a bit out of shape or your hair needs a trim – but that's as far as it should go. If these photos make you feel totally unattractive and unhappy it's time to get a grip on how unimportant and unrealistic these so-called perfect bodies really are.

*"The first time someone called me a beefcake –
I almost threw up."*
Tom Cruise

THE FOOD AND FITNESS FACTOR

Most of us eat too many highly processed foods which contain far too much fat, as well as too much sugar and salt. A healthy diet should be rich in fresh vegetables and fruit, eaten raw, boiled or microwaved; bread and cereals – preferably whole-grain; white meat – such as pork and skinless chicken; and fresh fish, but not the kind that comes deep-fried in batter from the chip shop.

Bad eating habits often start when you are a child. If you have always snacked on crisps, chocolate and fizzy drinks it seems daft to stop when you're a teenager and feeling full of life. But you could be storing up problems such as obesity, diabetes and heart disease in later life.

There's no need to be obsessive and boring about your food; healthy eating is more about getting a good balance between junk food and nourishing food. Start noticing how often you eat high-fat foods – anything fried, meat without the fat cut off, crisps, butter, cakes and biscuits, and if it's more than your consumption of healthy meals it's time to change the balance.

The Low Fat File

1) If your school lunches only consist of chips and fast food, try to spend some of your dinner money in advance and bring in a healthy sandwich and piece of fruit to school every other day instead.

2) When making a sandwich you can cut down on the fat without even noticing – if it's mayonnaise you fancy why add butter as well? You can halve the fat content by leaving it out, it won't taste any different. Similarly with peanut butter, you don't need peanut butter and butter in the same sandwich.

3) If you rush out of the house without your breakfast, you'll be down the sweet shop by break time. Pack in the sweets and crisps and have a decent breakfast instead – there are some brilliant cereals about that are quick and easy to eat.

4) Don't feel as though you have to plough your way through a meal just because it's dinner time. Eat what you need to feel satisfied and stop there. But be sure to eat a little bit of everything instead of just the food you like and leaving all the vegetables!

5) Don't worry if you have a pig-out day, just make sure you pay special attention to what you eat the rest of the week to make up for it.

6) Drink plenty of water – it's good for you as well as filling you up. If you fancy a change, opt for a calorie-free soft drink instead.

7) Eat slowly! Research proves that skinnies eat much more slowly that fatties.

8) Always go for a whole sweet thing like a chocolate bar or a couple of biscuits, rather than nibbling at a packet of sweets all afternoon – you'll never feel satisfied and it's much worse for your teeth.

9) Try to eat your evening meal at least two hours before you go to bed, so that you give yourself a chance to burn off some of the calories.

10) Finally, using food as a treat will make you think that keeping in shape should be a punishment. The treat yourself, starve yourself style of eating is a trap that will leave you feeling miserable, fat and ugly. If you eat sensibly and healthily, you won't need to think about dieting and food won't be a constant battle with your

conscience. If you want to treat yourself, don't do it with a Big Mac meal, buy a new T-shirt instead!

Fighting Fit

Physical exercise is a wonderful way of relieving stress, whether it's a long walk or a strenuous game of football. Sport is a great safety valve for stress – as long as you don't take it too seriously so that it gives you even more stress!

Fitness is vitally important for a healthy, fulfilled life. Exercise develops the health of the heart and lungs, strengthens the bones and muscles and is excellent for both physical and emotional health, and tones and shapes the body.

But it's no use doing work-outs unless you're holding yourself correctly first – bad posture will eventually cause you terrible discomfort. In any physical training you should make sure your body is in the correct position so that you benefit from the exercise.

If you're feeling down and sluggish, physical activity will do more to lift your mood than staying slumped in front of the TV. Equally though, after a long, action-packed day don't push your body and moods too far – you'll only end up irritable. Instead, never underestimate the benefits of a good night's sleep!

STAND TO ATTENTION

Good posture might take a bit of effort initially; it's very easy to fall into bad habits. If you're taller than everyone else you might be used to rounding your shoulders to look smaller. If you feel shy or unconfident it's easy to slouch. Many people sit sloppily at their desk. Do any of these sound familiar? If so, now is the time to change, as good posture will not only give you strength, stamina and suppleness, it will also improve your looks immediately.

Stand naked in front of a full-length mirror, turn your whole body to the side and close your eyes. Let your body relax into your normal posture. When ready, open your eyes and turn only your head to the mirror. Has your neck collapsed or have your shoulders curved foward? Is your back tortuously bent, with your bottom and tummy sticking out?

If any or all of these are true you are not alone, but you do desperately need to put your body back in line. Think: neck long, neck free, shoulders down, shoulders back. Think: back wider, back straight. Your shoulder and hip bones should be in a straight line with each other which means tucking your stomach and bottom in! Your feet should be pointed straight ahead, not pigeon-toed. Let yourself relax by breathing deeply in your new posture and try to practise so it soon becomes second nature.

Standing well is standing tall. Good posture could instantly add a couple of extra inches to your height – which is always attractive. Even if you're tall and self-conscious about your height, you will always look better if you stand well.

DEODORANTS AND ANTI-PERSPIRANTS

We all know that exercise makes us sweat, so taking a shower after playing any sports is the logical thing to do. But during puberty you don't even need to have been running around to find that you're suffering from a bad case of BO – the dreaded Body Odour. You can feel hot under the collar by simply having a laugh with your mates or getting worked up over an exam.

As your body develops it kick-starts your two and a half million sweat glands into action. It's not at all unusual to start having sweaty feet, palms, genitals and of course underarms – these are the places where there are a great many sweat glands and that's why it gets so stinky.

Sweating is your body's natural way to cool down but, surprisingly, sweat itself has no smell of its own. It's the stale bacteria left on the surface of your skin that causes sweat to smell when it dries. Your stale body odour is deeply unpleasant for everyone around you, but unfortunately the strong smell of BO is quite difficult to detect on yourself!

After a long day, if you still think you smell quite fresh, try sniffing the underarms of a close-fitting shirt or T-shirt that you were wearing. If this reeks of BO, there is no getting away from it, you probably do too.

Keeping your arms down all day or spraying deodorant over the top of the smell to disguise it is not going to make any difference – remember, other people will still be able to smell it even if you think you have cleverly masked it.

To keep BO at bay requires a simple but regular hygiene routine. Wash your armpits every day, either in the shower or at the basin. Make sure they are washed with soap and then rinse with warm, clean water. Pat dry with a clean towel, making sure that the towel still smells clean afterwards.

Use a deodorant or anti-perspirant straight away and leave this to dry for a couple of minutes on your skin before getting dressed, otherwise it will get rubbed off onto your clothing, leaving you unprotected.

What are the differences between deodorants and anti-perspirants? Deodorants won't stop you sweating, but they do contain chemicals which neutralise the bacteria on your skin so it won't create a bad smell. Anti-perspirants actually aim to dry out the sweat glands, so that less sweat is produced.

You can buy both products in stick form, as a roll-on or in a spray can, and although they are equally effective they need to be washed off and re-applied every day as their effect quickly wears off, especially after an active or hot day.

SKIN IRRITATION

Leaving a wound dry and exposed to air speeds healing and decreases the risk of further infection.

It also reduces itching. Drying with a blow-dryer for ten to 15 minutes is roughly the equivalent of a day's worth of air exposure so you can shorten the healing time considerably. Thoroughly cleanse the wound with soap and water, gently patting off any excess water before using the dryer. Set the dryer to the lowest setting, preferably cold, and always keep it at least ten inches away from your skin.

HANDS, FEET AND NAILS

Those bits that stick out on the ends of your limbs can often make you feel quite awkward and gangly but you really need your hands and feet, so taking extra time to care for them properly won't be time wasted.

Handy Hints

Try to protect your hands whenever possible. This means wearing rubber gloves when you do the washing-up! Make extra effort during the winter to protect against chapped skin, which is when your hands feel sore and look red and cracked. To prevent this complaint, wear gloves when you are outdoors and try not to expose your hands to extreme changes in temperature.

Apply a rich moisturising hand cream to keep the skin supple every once in a while – Vaseline is one

YOUR BODY AND OTHER BITS

of the simplest and best products for hands. While putting it on, give your hands a massage at the same time – take each finger and knead it with the thumb and first finger of the other hand. Continue this all over your hands and finish by shaking and circling the wrists. Because your hands are great tension and stress holders, these exercises will really help you to relax before an important date or event.

Heel and Toe Tips

It's surprisingly easy to get your feet into shape even if you have been ignoring them lately. They do deserve the occasional spot of attention as they walk an average of 15,000 steps a day.

If you thought your armpits were smelly – wait for this. There are more sweat glands on the soles of your feet than on any other part of your body! So it's crucial that you wash your feet every day. Use a small nail brush to remove the dirt from between your toes and under the nails. A piece of pumice stone is perfect for getting rid of a build-up of hard skin on your heels or the balls of your feet.

It's most important to dry your feet really thoroughly before encasing them in shoes and socks for the day. Take time to work the towel between each toe and finish by dusting with a little talcum powder to keep them feeling dry and cool.

Whenever possible, give your feet a regular airing by walking around barefoot. Trainers are designed to let your feet breathe, but unless they are made entirely of leather, your feet will soon feel hot and sweaty if you wear them day in and day out. Try to vary your footwear; your feet will really benefit from a regular change. And always change your socks every day – turning them inside out won't do!

Problem Feet

Feet can be prone to a lot of unattractive problems but the majority of them can be avoided by washing and drying them regularly and by not wearing ill-fitting shoes. Corns and blisters, although not very traumatic, are often quite painful but they can be treated easily with corn plasters or a little antiseptic cream.

Athlete's foot is a widely used term for any fungal infection which affects the skin between the toes. It can be tricky to treat, as the condition of your feet for most of the time is hot, moist and enclosed – which is ideal for any kind of fungus to flourish. These are also ripe conditions for the growth of a verruca, which is a kind of wart on the sole of your foot.

In-growing toenails can be agonisingly painful, and usually result from having cut the toenails incorrectly. You must cut them straight across, not curved around.

With all these problems, seek medical help early on for proper advice and treatment.

Treats for Feet

Get into the habit of exercising your feet whenever you are sitting for any length of time. Rubbing them, making small circles with your thumb, will help boost circulation in your feet and legs. Policemen don't rise up and down on the balls of their feet for nothing – it exercises the foot and calf muscles, which is ideal if you have to stand for long periods of time.

Really flex your feet by trying to pick up a pencil with your toes, or try sitting on the end of the bed and carefully roll an empty, chilled milk bottle backwards and forwards under your foot for a very effective prevention and cure for cramp.

After a really strenuous day, treat your feet to an aromatic foot soak. Prepare two bowls, one with hot water containing half a cup of salt to revive and clean the feet, and the other with cold water with the juice of a lemon added to soften the feet. Put your feet in the hot water for five minutes and then into the cold for one minute and repeat a couple of times. Your feet will feel fresh, revived and ready for action!

Natty Nails

While you are stuck with the shape and size of your hands, you can still change their appearance by keeping a check on the condition of your nails. It might seem like wasted time and effort looking after your nails as nice nails on boys are rarely commented on, but it's a fact that when your nails look bad – everybody notices.

If you find your fingernails are always chipped and jagged it's probably because you treat them too roughly. Keep them short by trimming them in a slight curve with sharp nail scissors or clippers. You will never achieve an even line or smooth finish if you use ordinary scissors.

Strong, naturally glossy nails are a sign of good health, while flaky nails with small white flecks or horizontal ridges on the surface might occur because you are not eating a balanced diet. Strengthen your nails by eating more calcium, the mineral that is found in meat, milk, cheese, eggs and fish. A daily diet of one or more of these ingredients is essential for making strong bones and nails.

Nail Nibblers

Nail biting is a nervous habit which leaves your fingers feeling tender and sore and makes you look nervy and anxious. It's not very good for you either, as dirt collects behind nails. Instead, make a confident impression by breaking this habit now.

You can buy a revolting tasting clear nail polish to paint onto your nails to help you keep them away from your mouth. But you must re-apply a new coat every time you wash, otherwise the nasty taste quickly wears off – making it easy to cheat. How about getting a member of the family to sponsor you not to bite your nails for a month – everyone likes a challenge. Double the incentive to quit by saying you will pay the same sum of money to them if you fail!

TATTOO YOU

Choosing to have a tattoo should be a carefully considered decision and not done as a macho dare set up by your mates. For a start, it's illegal to get a tattoo done before you're 18 so if you know a parlour that will do one for you before that age you should be very wary about what other risks they are prepared to take with your body.

The most serious risk people getting a tattoo should consider is blood-borne infections such as hepatitis B and HIV. Tattoo needles are not disposable and, although tattoo artists are recommended to use proper steam sterilisers, many still use chemical and ultrasonic cleaners which are not as effective in killing infectious germs.

The image is fixed in the skin by the formation of microscopic scars, which can be a bloody and painful experience as your skin is being punctured by multiple needle pricks. After the tattoo is completed, a scab builds up over the injured skin

but this heals and falls off within a week or so –
much as when you badly graze your knee.

Be quite sure who you are getting a tattoo for.
Your current girlfriend might think it's dead sexy
and attractive but your future girlfriend might find
it a complete turn-off, so if you do decide you want
a tattoo, make sure it's a design you choose and
really want.

EAR PIERCING

Ear piercing has been popular with men and women
since the early Bronze Age – for over 4000 years –
so it's a little surprising that some people still find it
shocking or unusual. Boys especially can be frowned
upon if they consider having their ears pierced.
This is because in relatively recent history, earrings
on boys represented rebellion. Traditionally, it was
only pirates and ex-convicts who were the type to
sport an earring, so some parents and schools feel
an earring will put you at a disadvantage when you
need to be seen as responsible – such as at an
interview for a job or work experience.

You can't change their attitude, just as you
wouldn't want them to try to change yours, so if
you find you are up against heavy opposition you
will have to wait until you are of an age to make all
your own decisions. It might seem like forever, but

considering that you have the rest of your adult life to live the way you wish, your teenage years are a relatively short time.

Never attempt to pierce your own ear. The chance of getting an infection is very high. This will mean you have to take the earring out, which means the hole will probably close up, so it totally defeats the whole purpose. Nor is it more manly or brave to pierce your own ear, as everyone who's had it done knows it doesn't really hurt anyway.

Instead, go to a reputable ear-piercing centre – they are often attached to hairdressing salons, but check your local Yellow Pages. Your ear should be pierced with an ear-piercing gun which fires a special sterilised piercing stud through your lobe. This earring should be brand new and the post made of solid gold.

You should keep this stud in for a minimum of six weeks and turn the earring every day with clean hands – never fiddle with it otherwise. Ask the piercer what they recommend to keep it clean, but most will say dab with diluted surgical spirit on cotton wool to keep any infection away.

COSMETIC SURGERY

"*I wish I had my old face back.*"
Michael Jackson

The stage between puberty and adulthood is a very insecure time for everyone as it's a time when your body is changing the most. Of course there are going to be bits that will make you feel unhappy. The thing to remember is that the bit you hate this year might make you feel quite proud next year.

There are all sorts of stories from America of school kids having surgery to keep up with the latest trend, but it's one of those things that could only happen in America. British cosmetic surgeons simply wouldn't allow it. While your body is still growing and developing it's ridiculous to be put under pressure to look a certain way because while you're a teenager you can never be sure of how you're eventually going to feel about your appearance later in life.

These days, cosmetic surgery is available to virtually everyone who has the money, and in some deserving cases – like after a road accident – treatment can be obtained free on the NHS. Vanity is not usually considered a deserving case unless you have a very noticeable disfigurement.

In a society where people take their bodies very seriously, it's natural to want to go as far as you can to achieve perfection. But you need to be realistic too – perfection is never possible. Even a cosmetic surgeon cannot guarantee that the results will be just what you wanted. Most surgeons will require you to have some counselling before any operation to be sure that you aren't expecting a new shape of nose to bring you love, happiness or success – because it won't.

And remember, cosmetic surgery is just like any other surgery; it involves a certain amount of risk, so it is most important to check that your surgeon has comprehensive insurance just in case something does go wrong.

Chapter Nine

FASHION AND STYLE

It's easy to think that fashion and style are much the same thing, but this is just not the case. A fashionable outfit is one that is being promoted and hyped to the hilt as this year's look. Anyone with enough money can buy it and walk out of the shop confident that they are keeping up with the current trends.

Someone with style, on the other hand, has that indefinable quality that's practically impossible to copy perfectly as it is unique to that individual. Having true style is being one step ahead of the game – starting trends, not following them.

It's the unexpected quality that makes style so surprising and difficult to describe – putting layers and colours together in a way that no one would have thought of but still making it work.

Having such confidence with your clothes is a very rare talent indeed. The vast majority of us have days when we feel like our clothes are wearing us instead of the other way round. It's that feeling of having nothing to wear when you've got a cupboard crammed full of clothes or you catch sight of your reflection and you look nothing like you hoped or imagined.

It is especially difficult if you're in a growing spurt and one bit is ahead of the rest or there is a particular look you'd love to get into but money is holding you back. Don't let these difficulties stop you doing the things you want to – it's the experience of playing the sport that's important, not owning the complete kit, or going to the dance club even if you're lacking trendy labels.

The best compliment anyone can pay to you is not to admire your jacket or new boots, but to make a spontaneous comment like 'You look brilliant.' Then you know you've got it right.

WHERE TO START

The first place to start to gain any kind of individual style is to take control of what clothes you wear. If your mum is prepared to buy you some new clothes – go with her! Don't just wait to see what she brings home in the hope that you'll like it.

Start finding out what suits you by spending some time in the shops trying different clothes on. If this sounds like a nightmare it's probably because the last time you did any serious shopping was the

Saturday before Christmas – which is a nightmare for everyone. Boys who don't do their own clothes shopping miss out on learning to look and picking up a good sense of visual awareness.

Go easy on yourself – always avoid the centre of town for clothes shopping at the weekend. Instead, go on a Monday afternoon during half-term, or in the holidays, when the assistants are less harassed and have time to help.

Are your clothes appropriate for your current lifestyle and right for the shape of your body now?

Take a proper look at all your clothes and pull out anything that you haven't worn for the past year. This excludes special occasion wear – like a smart suit which you only reserve for specific events.

If you haven't worn an item of casual wear for over a year it's unlikely that you'll ever wear it again, so it's time to stop giving it valuable wardrobe or drawer space. This is not to imply that everything you own has to be a recent purchase. You may well have owned several garments for some years that you are still wearing regularly.

The right clothes can boost your confidence, but similarly, the wrong ones can take it away. Never wear anything that gives you a fogey feeling. If you feel dreary in grey or subdued in wishy-washy shades, then avoid these colours. In fact, any clothes that make you feel fed-up instead of ready-to-go are best got rid of as quickly as possible.

THE BASICS

Jeans, chinos, jogging bottoms, shorts, T-shirts, check shirts, denim shirts, polo shirts, sweatshirts.

Your basics are your standard tops and trousers that can be intermixed in many different ways. Never spend huge amounts of money on your basics. They are there to be washed, worn and replaced with a reasonable amount of frequency. Jeans are the one exception – they can be washed and worn and washed and worn until they are like a second skin. Because their lifespan is longer, spending a bit more on them is still cost-effective.

The basics in your wardrobe are the very bits that you build several outfits from. For instance, your jeans can go with any number of tops, just as a white T-shirt is good for a crisp smart look or a slob on the sofa look. Casual, informal wear for boys has really developed in the last few years – but it still needs planning to get it right.

Your basics will be at their most valuable and versatile if you choose them in plain fabrics – like pure cotton in a plain colour. If you crave variety, look at checks or stripes which won't date. The principal standard you should set for all your casual clothes is that they should be like old friends – the first thing you reach for.

T-shirts

T-shirts have been used to promote everything from world peace to Pepsi-Cola. If you let them, advertisers will use your chest as a walking billboard for any old product. Unless your dad owns the company, avoid advertising slogans and logos on your basic T-shirts, as they can make you look like you haven't got a mind of your own and the design might not look good under a shirt or jacket.

Promotional T-shirts for bands have always been most popular with boys – with heavy metal T-shirts selling more than any other music style. These types of T-shirt are great as long as they're not the only ones you've got. Nothing can beat the classic, plain black or white cotton T-shirt for versatility.

Buy at least one to look fresh in every summer – you'll be surprised how the shape and style of a classic T-shirt does regularly change. From XXXL and baggy to torso-hugging and tight, long-sleeved, cap-sleeved, sleeveless, ribbed or cropped, this year's shape added to your old faithful jeans will instantly bring a classic combination right up to date.

Jeans and Denim Jackets

Traditionally, denim was designed for workwear. It's the ideal fabric – it's tough and hard-wearing but still soft and comfortable, the colour doesn't run and it never shrinks out of all proportion. That's the reason everybody loves it.

Before buying a new pair of jeans, you should have an idea of what sort you want before you go shopping. Styles vary ever so slightly, so after having tried on six similar pairs you'll be too confused to make a decision. Do you want black, blue, white or a fashion colour; zip or button fly; drainpipe or baggy fit? Tell the assistant your basic requirements. Denim jackets need to be roomy enough to be able to wear a thick brushed cotton shirt underneath without being baggy round the waist.

Wash denim inside-out for an even fade, especially black jeans that are prone to going streaky. If you want to keep that deep black shade, top up the colour with a packet of machine home dye. One box will do one pair of jeans and no, it won't wreck the washing machine, but you do need to follow the instructions carefully to avoid any dyeing disasters.

Never throw jeans away even if they don't fit you. If they've got too short in the leg, chop them into cut-offs so they're either knee or thigh length. You don't even need to hem them – a few raw threads hanging down makes the ideal finish. Save the leg piece that you've cut off – denim is an ideal fabric for patches. Is your denim jacket too short in the sleeve? Cut off both arms at the seam for a classic waistcoat to be worn over long-sleeved T-shirts, brushed cotton shirts or under or over a leather biker jacket.

EXTRAS

Baseball caps, hats, sunglasses, watches, badges, rings, belts, braces, ties, dungarees, waistcoats, leather jackets and leather jeans, silk shirts, suits.

Extras add that extra something to your overall look. Choose one or several to give a stamp of individuality to your basic wardrobe. You can be a bit bolder with the design of extras as you won't be wanting to wear them all the time. Become known for having great taste in waistcoats, second-hand suits or unusual belt buckles. Whatever you choose, make it your own by wearing it with confidence.

Imitation is the sincerest form of flattery, so wait for your mates to copy your look before abandoning it. Developing a personal style takes time, so don't be afraid to wear the same look several times – it'll show that you are sure of how good it looks!

Never be afraid to layer your look. In the spring and autumn, dispense with a jacket by wearing several soft layers instead. Try a T-shirt with a checked shirt over the top. Wear a denim shirt open over the top of that. Push the sleeves up and tie a sweatshirt round your waist for good measure. You'll soon develop a good eye for what patterns and colours mix well – look at tartan, several colours blended successfully on one fabric.

KNITWEAR

Jumpers, sweaters, pullovers, cardigans, tank tops,

Argyll, Aran, Guernsey, chunky, flecked, oiled wool, lambswool, ski style, fisherman style, V-necked, crew-necked, cotton-knit, hand-knit.

Knitwear is a tricky one, as the best knitwear is made of pure wool, but pure wool is rarely machine-washable so your best jumper might spend most of its life in the dirty washing bin waiting to be hand-washed – especially if it's pale. They also need to be handled with care and washed with a gentle non-biological powder or liquid and dried flat.

Buying the best knitwear often means you are buying a lot of bother, but this is not meant to put you off. Pure new wool beats 100 per cent acrylic every time. Take your time when choosing knitwear, as there are some decent machine-washable wool jumpers to be found.

When buying a new jumper it's rarely wise to buy your exact size. If it's a chunky style you're going for and you usually wear a medium, try on a large or even an extra-large and see how it looks. Chunky knitwear is supposed to look big and soft, just baggy will not do! The same goes for a fine knit jumper. If it's supposed to look slim and lean, you don't want folds of fabric hanging round your waist – try one size down for a snug fit.

SOCKS AND UNDERWEAR

Boxers, Y-fronts, underpants, briefs, trunks, vest and brief sets, all-in-ones, sports socks, country socks, slim-fit socks, coloured and patterned socks.

The design of boxer shorts, naturally enough, was taken from the boxing ring. Boxer shorts, along with the similarly sport-inspired singlet, first appeared in the 1930s. In 1946 the traditional Y-front briefs swept the shops with an advertising slogan that proclaimed them to be 'scientifically perfected for correct masculine support'.

For many years to follow, the boys' and men's underwear market lay dormant – it was as though the classic white boxer and Y-front could never be improved upon. The seventies dallied with a synthetic version, and for a while nylon Union Jack underpants were IT. Then with the 1980s came Sex Appeal. The magazines were full of pop stars and male models stripping down to reveal a new wave of designer underwear and all young blood after that felt obliged to follow suit.

The boom years have moved on but the male underwear market will never be the same again. Boys are now more confident in choosing their own boxers and briefs, which can only be a good thing as they do cover one of their most prized possessions!

The selection is wide and varied, catering for all tastes and comforts. The classic woven boxer has still survived but it can now be seen sporting anything from Disney characters to the Paisley print. However, it's the jersey boxer that's making major sales. Jersey is a knitted fabric – it's the same stuff that T-shirts are made from. Therefore you are getting more support and comfort than you do with the traditional woven boxer. With the introduction of lycra into underwear, you can now also enjoy all the comfort and benefits of stretch. Silk boxers are always sensuous and particularly prevalent around Christmas and Valentine's Day. And now, with the development of machine-washable silk, there's no need to reserve them for special occasions. The Y-front design has been brought completely up-to-date and can now be found on jersey boxers, briefs and trunks.

Buying a new pair of briefs is not a huge investment, so treat yourself once in a while to a new shape or style. Only you can decide which design you find the most comfortable and flattering.

There can be no excuses for not changing your socks every day, and considering how sweaty your feet get it's crucial that your socks are made from at least 50 per cent cotton. Synthetic socks should be a mistake of the past.

The weave on a sock has to be quite tight in order to fit your foot snugly, but if your feet are on a growing spurt the size of your socks should be too. Socks are stretchy so it's easy to squeeze your foot into a size that's too small, but ultimately your feet will suffer. So, stock up on new socks for your new size.

SHOES, BOOTS AND TRAINERS

Wellies, sandals, trainers, ankle boots, brogues, slip-ons, slippers, cowboy boots, work boots, hiking boots, deck shoes, loafers, lace-ups.

When it comes to footwear, boys have always been the lucky ones. No cramming feet into crippling stilettos for you. But with girls now demanding fashionable boots and sturdy shoes of their own, boys have also benefited, as the choice of styles for both sexes has never been better. Once, brogues or lace-up shoes were a necessity for a formal look but the classic eight or ten hole work boot has now become so commonplace that it can look equally smart.

Choosing new shoes or boots is a complicated business and shouldn't be embarked upon lightly. Footwear has always been expensive and if you wear a pair once or twice and find they don't fit after all – you're lumbered with them. No shoe shop will have them back and they're useless to you.

Don't be pressured into buying a mistake because the shop assistant looks tired or harassed or says your size is out of stock. Say you'll wait for another delivery or see if they can be ordered from another branch. While your feet are still growing they need to be measured every time you consider buying footwear.

Just because you are a certain size in one shop, don't assume that this is your size for every shop. Lots of shoes are made abroad and show the continental sizes only. Always try on shoes with the type of socks you would normally wear them with. Try and buy shoes in the afternoon when your feet have swelled to their largest.

You might have heard that trainers are bad for your feet, but if they are made of leather they're no different from any leather shoe. Whatever style you choose, it's important that your big toe is straight and not pinched or curved, and the shoe is secure but not tight. Feet need a good airing as often as possible, so get into the habit of wearing slip-ons or deck shoes with bare feet on a hot summer's day.

BARGAIN TACTICS

At sale time you can undoubtedly pick up a few bargains but you can end up just as easily with a few impulsive mistakes and it's almost impossible to exchange goods that are bought in sales. Surviving the sales takes all your shopping skills.

1) Do look through your cupboard before you leave home to remind yourself of what you actually need.

2) Do check that your garment hasn't been marked down due to rips, stains or faults that cannot be repaired or hidden.

3) Do always try things on before buying.

4) Do think about the money you're paying out, NOT the money you're saving. It's easy to be enticed by a big reduction.

5) Finally, DON'T go anywhere near the sales if you're flat broke!

Chapter Ten

YOU KNOW YOUR EFFORTS HAVE PAID OFF WHEN ...

Her best friend walks into the classroom and she doesn't bother going to speak to her ...

Everyone races for the back of the bus and she races ahead to ensure she gets a seat near to you ...

She offers you the whole bag when you only asked for one crisp ...

She asks you what sun sign you are ...

She laughs at all your jokes even when you fluff the punchline ...

She says she's doing 'nothing special' for the whole of the summer holidays ...

She happens to love all the bands you say you like...

She asks if there are any more Saturday jobs where you work ...

She knows where you live without you ever having told her ...

Her friends do a lot of nudge-nudge, wink-winking when you walk into the classroom ...

She puts your telephone number in her address book ...

Index